P9-DEL-741

WOODY WOODPECKER

AMAZING ANIMAL WORLDS

BELINDA WEBER

CONTENTS

Project Manager: Belinda Weber
Art Editor: Eljay Yildirim
Coordinating Editor: Sarah Snavely
Designer: Dean Price
DTP Manager: Nicky Studdart
Production Controller: Jo Blackmore

KINGFISHER/UNIVERSAL
Larousse Kingfisher Chambers Inc.
80 Maiden Lane
New York, New York 10038
www.kingfisherpub.com

First published in 2002

10 9 8 7 6 5 4 3 2 1

1TR/1201/TWP/MAR(MAR)/130SINAR

Copyright © Kingfisher Publications Plc 2002

Woody Woodpecker™ and Friends is a trademark and copyright of Walter Lantz Productions, Inc. Licensed by Universal Studios Licensing, Inc. All rights reserved.

All rights reserved under International and Pan-American Copyright Conventions

LIBRARY OF CONGRESS CATALOGING-IN-PUBLICATION DATA has been applied for.

ISBN 0-7534-5518-8

Printed in Singapore

Woody Woodpecker™ is going on vacation, and he wants to look up some old friends along the way. He's decided to visit them in their homes and check out where they all live.

Woody™ has friends all over the place—some live on islands, some in huge rain forests, some in the oceans, and others in the dry, sandy desert. He knows that all his animal friends have different ways of adapting to the places in which they live, and he wants to find out more. Woody™ wants to know how some animals survive in the desert and how others manage to live their whole lives in the seas.

Life in a forest

Some forest trees lose their leaves in the winter. These are known as deciduous forests. Woody™ has many friends that live in these forests. They make their homes both in the trees and on the ground.

STEALTHY HUNTERS

Lynx are shy creatures that live in forests or places with lots of cover. In the dappled light their spotted coats make them difficult to see.

Wacky World

Deer are the only animals in the world with antlers, which the males grow every year. Male deer lock antlers with each other when they are fighting over territory or females. Occasionally they even get stuck!

SCENT MARKING

Deer mark trees at the edge of their home territory with a strong scent that keeps other deer away.

SILENT FLIGHT
Barn owls have soft feathers that help them fly silently through the air to catch their prey.

CLIMBING TREES
Squirrels are excellent climbers. They have sharp claws for running up and down trees.

Forests at night
Badgers, bats, hedgehogs, and owls all live in deciduous forests. They come out at night to feed. Badgers live in holes in the ground called setts. They eat worms and small rodents.

Lakes and rivers

Many animals live in or next to rivers and lakes. Some can only live in the water, while others survive just as well on dry land. Otters live in holes in the riverbank. They love playing and sliding down the muddy banks into the water. Woody™ thinks this looks like fun, but doesn't want to get his feathers too muddy and wet!

MESSY SWANS
Mute swans lay their eggs in scruffy nests of twigs and leaves built among reeds at the water's edge.

Kingfishers use their beaks and claws to dig a nest burrow in the riverbanks. They are sloppy birds, and their nests quickly become cluttered with smelly fish bones and droppings.

CARING FATHERS

Unlike other fish that just release their eggs into the water, male sticklebacks make a cozy nest from plants for them. The male fish then guards the eggs and young. After about two weeks the young swim away and start a life on their own.

LIVING ON LAND AND WATER

Newts live in water and in damp places on land. In the water they eat tadpoles and insects. On the land they catch slugs and worms.

FEATHERED FUN!

What's the difference between a bird and a fly? A bird can fly, but a fly can't bird!

FEATHERED FUN!

What fish do dogs chase? Catfish.

Swamps and wetlands

Swamps and marshes are types of wetlands. The ground is always under water or very soggy. Wading birds, such as the roseate spoonbill of the southern U.S., have longer legs than Woody™, so they can stand up in shallow water. They feed by swinging their bills through the water, taking in anything they can eat.

NOISY TRUMPETER
The rare whooping crane of North America gets its name from its loud call. It sounds like a high-pitched trumpeting.

TURNING TURTLE
Terrapins are small turtles that live in or near water. They eat plants or other animals such as snails and worms.

Wacky World

Fiddler crabs live in wetlands and mangrove swamps. The males have one small claw and one huge one that they wave at other males to keep them away from their territory.

BIG BIRD
The wood stork is one of America's largest flying birds. It lives near water where it catches fish to eat. Wood storks make large nests of sticks in treetops.

WATCHING WATER
Little green herons wait beside shallow water for their prey. They eat fish, frogs, and small mammals.

EAT LIKE AN ALLIGATOR?
Alligators live in rivers and swamps where they feed on anything they catch, from birds to turtles!

Sharks in the shallows

Sharks are the sea's best-known hunters. Woody™ is amazed at how fast they can swim and how their excellent sense of smell helps them find the tiniest morsels of food. Sand tiger sharks have several rows of scary-looking teeth in their mouths. They hunt fish and other sea creatures.

CORAL PATROL
Blacktip reef sharks live at the edges of the coral reefs, hunting the animals that live there.

BIG MOUTH
The great white is the largest hunting shark. Its huge mouth bites chunks out of seals and dolphins as well as other fish.

A hammer for a head?

Hammerhead sharks look like typical sharks until you see their heads, which are a strange T-shape with one eye at each end. No one knows exactly why their heads are like this, but Woody™ thinks it helps them hunt fish.

SLEEPY ZEBRAS

Young zebra sharks have stripes on their backs, but the adults have brown spots. Zebra sharks rest near the bottom of coral reefs by day, but hunt at night.

FEATHERED FUN!
What do you get
from a bad-tempered shark?
As far away as possible!

FEATHERED FUN!
Why did the shark
want to become a carpenter?
Because he was a hammerhead!

Whales and dolphins

Although whales and dolphins look like fish, Woody™ knows that they are warm-blooded mammals that spend their whole lives in the water. They breathe air, so they have to come to the surface regularly. Killer whales are fast swimmers and can jump high out of the water. They live in most of the world's oceans.

GENTLE GIANT

Blue whales are the biggest animals ever known. Adults can be up to 100 ft. (30m) long. These monster mammals swim through the Arctic and Antarctic oceans, eating tiny krill and plankton.

Dancing dolphins

Dolphins are fast-swimming, playful animals that often leap right out of the water. This is called porpoising. Dolphins are intelligent and sociable animals that live in groups called pods.

JUMPING WHALES

Southern right whales live in the open oceans. They leap out of the water and fall back with a huge splash. This is called breaching. Don't get wet, Woody™!

Wacky World

The blue whale is so long that eight adult elephants could stand on its back. This mighty mammal is also a heavyweight. It weighs the same as 150 cars!

13

Island life

Animals that live on islands are separated from the mainland. They may look or behave differently from their relatives living in other places. Many of the animals living on the Galapagos Islands in the Pacific Ocean, including the Galapagos penguins, are only found there. Woody™ recognizes some of them, but others look completely new to him!

WEIGHTY GIANTS

Galapagos giant tortoises have extra-long necks for stretching to reach tasty morsels of cacti and other plants. They can weigh up to 770 lbs (350kg).

Wacky World

All the animals and plants that live on the Galapagos Islands are protected. The islands themselves have been turned into a huge national park.

FLYING PIRATES

Frigatebirds are the pirates of the air. If they spot another bird with a fish, they snap at it until the bird drops its catch. The frigatebird then swoops down and swallows the fish.

SWIMMING LIZARDS

Marine iguanas are the only lizards that regularly swim in the sea. They live on rocky shores, but go into the water to eat seaweed. They have to cling onto the rocks so that they don't get washed away.

HELPFUL CRABS

Red crabs scuttle over iguanas resting on the rocks, eating any blood-sucking ticks that are on their skin.

Amazing Amazon

Rain forests are packed with life as Woody™ is finding out. They contain about three quarters of all the known species of plants and animals. In the Amazon rain forest of South America spider monkeys hang from the trees. They are the most acrobatic of all the monkeys, using their tails as easily as their hands or feet.

UP IN THE TREES
Jaguars often rest in trees during the heat of the day. Their spotted coats help them hide in the dappled light of the forest.

LIVING IN TROOPS
Squirrel monkeys are sociable animals that live in large troops of up to 500 individuals. They cannot grip with their tails, but use them for balance when running along high branches.

Ferocious fish

The Amazon River is home to many fish. Red piranhas live in large schools and are hunters that eat the flesh of other animals. They will even attack and eat large land animals that get stranded in the water.

DOZY MANATEE
Manatees spend their days dozing near the river's surface. They wake at night to eat.

HEAVYWEIGHT SNAKES
The anaconda is one of the world's longest and heaviest snakes. It catches animals that come to the water to drink and squeezes them to death.

Tropical rain forest

Rain forests are bursting with life, and the southeast Asian ones are no exception. Everywhere Woody™ looks he can see strange and fascinating creatures. The male Count Raggi's bird of paradise uses its colorful feathers to put on a spectacular display to attract a female.

BIGGEST BUTTERFLY
Birdwing butterflies are among the largest of all. This rare Queen Alexandra's birdwing butterfly comes from Papua New Guinea and grows to 11 in. (28cm) across.

FOXES THAT FLY?

Flying foxes are fruit bats. They have large eyes and can see in the dark. They leave their forest homes at night to feast on rain forest fruit. They are very messy eaters. They squash fruit in their mouths, drinking the juice but dropping the seeds and flesh onto the forest floor.

RARE RHINOCEROS

The Javan rhino lives in the forests of Indonesia and is the rarest large mammal in the world. Unlike other rhinos, Javan rhinos have little or no horns.

MAN OF THE FOREST

The word orangutan means "man of the forest" in the Malay language. This large ape has long, strong arms that it uses for climbing through the trees of its forest home. Orangutans don't like the rain. In storms they often use large leaves as umbrellas.

19

Life on the African plains

The African plains are wide and flat with plenty of grass to graze on. Lions doze under the few trees and bushes, while herds of antelope and other animals tuck into the green grass. Woody™ knows that the lions are on the lookout for something to hunt.

MIGHTY ELEPHANTS

African elephants are the largest land animals in the world. Their tusks can grow up to 10 ft. (3m) long.

SPOTTED HUNTERS

Leopards hunt their prey at night, sneaking up on their victims and attacking from close range. They are excellent climbers and will drag their kill into trees to stop scavengers from finding it. Leopards have between one and six cubs at a time.

STRIPED HORSES

Zebras are like horses with striped coats. They live in large herds on grasslands. No two zebras are exactly the same. Their stripes are always slightly different.

Wacky World

Ostriches are too big and heavy to fly. But they are very fast runners—they can run twice as fast as the fastest Olympic sprinters.

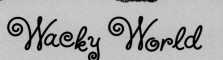

FEATHERED FUN!

Which takes less time to get ready for a trip, an elephant or a rooster? A rooster—he only takes his comb!

FEATHERED FUN!

Where do tough ostriches come from? Hard-boiled eggs!

Mountain life

Climbing up a mountainside, Woody™ is surprised to see how many animals live on the slopes. Andean condors are the world's largest flying birds. They are excellent fliers, soaring high above their mountain homes as they rise up on warm air currents called thermals.

EATING BAMBOO

Giant pandas live in the mountains of China. They eat all day, spending 10-12 hours a day feasting on bamboo.

LIVING IN THE SNOW

Yaks live in the highest region of the world—in the mountains of Tibet in Asia. Their woolly coats hang down around their knees, helping to keep them warm in the long, snowy winters.

Looking like a lion

Pumas are also called mountain lions, although they are not the same as lions. They have great strength and stamina, overpowering their prey by jumping on its back and biting its throat.

MOUNTAIN GOATS

Chamois are incredible mountaineers. They can run up almost sheer rock faces and jump from ledges with amazing ease.

LOOK OUT BELOW!

The lammergeier is a type of vulture. It eats the tough parts of dead animals, including the bones and skin. It smashes bones by dropping them when flying, so it can eat what's inside.

COLD CATERPILLARS

Unlike other butterflies, the Apollo copes well with the cold. The caterpillars hibernate during the winter and become butterflies in the spring.

SLEEPYHEADS

Marmots live in mountain pastures. They hibernate during the cold winters, sleeping for up to nine months of the year.

Evergreen forests

Evergreen forests grow in cold areas. Woody™ has found out that the trees keep their leaves in winter and provide cover year-round for the animals that live there. Elk make their homes in the forests, feeding on the leaves, buds, and bark of the trees.

BIG EATER!

The wolverine, or glutton, is famous for its huge appetite and strength. It is said to eat more than any other meat eater. It preys on other mammals and birds and will even drive bears away and steal their food.

LIVING ON NEEDLES

The capercaillie is a large forest bird. During the winter it survives by eating pine needles. The male capercaillie is over three feet (1m) long.

Woody™ likes to watch the male fan out its tail and raise its neck to attract a mate.

TWISTED BILL

The crossbill gets its name because the top and bottom parts of its beak cross over each other. This helps them pick the seeds out of pine and larch cones.

AGILE CLIMBER

Pine martens are excellent climbers, racing up and down trees with great ease. They are shy creatures that are usually only active at dusk or dawn when they hunt small mammals and birds or search for berries.

MIGHTY MOOSE

The moose is the largest living member of the deer family. It can grow 8 ft. (2.4m) tall. In the summer moose will wade into lakes to eat water plants.

FEATHERED FUN!
On which side does a bird have the most feathers?
On the outside!

FEATHERED FUN!
What animal do you look like in the bathtub?
A little bear!

Dry deserts

Deserts are very dry places where it hardly ever rains. Animals that live there have to survive on very little water. Deserts are so hot that many desert animals, including camel spiders, rest during the day and come out during the cooler nights. Woody™ didn't know that animals could live in such dry places.

Wacky World

Camels can fill up on water very quickly. They can drink over 25 gal. (100l) in just 10 minutes—that's the same as drinking a whole bathful of water.

NO WATER TO DRINK

Camels are known as the ships of the desert. They can last several days without water and can survive for weeks without a drink if they find enough green plants to eat.

26

SANDY FEET

Addax are rare antelope that live in small herds in the Sahara Desert. Their hooves are broad, allowing the addax to walk or run over the loose sand without sinking into it. They have an excellent sense of smell to help them find fresh grass.

HIDING IN THE SAND

Sand cats have yellowish-brown fur that helps them blend in with their sandy home. Their heads are broad and flat so they can peek around small rocks when hunting their prey.

LIZARDS WITH FRILLS

When it is frightened, the frilled lizard spreads its broad collar, making itself look bigger than it really is, and hisses. This scares away its enemies.

Summer in the Arctic

Woody™ can see that plenty of animals live in the icy Arctic. Many have their young during the brief summers, when plants grow and there is more food to eat. Snowy owls hunt lemmings on the open ground.

CHASING LEMMINGS

Wolves usually live in family groups, or packs, of up to 40 animals. Hunting as a pack, they can catch large animals, but they will also eat small creatures such as lemmings.

LOADS OF LEMMINGS

Lemmings are the most common mammal in the Arctic. Every few years they increase in number so much that there is not enough food for them all. Millions then set off to find new homes.

Digging for food

Walruses use their long front teeth to dig for shellfish on the seabed. The tusks are not long enough to dig with until the walrus is about two years old. Until then it stays with its mother and drinks her milk.

LONG-DISTANCE FLYERS

Snow geese breed in the Arctic. They spend the cold winters in Mexico, California, and Japan, flying back to breed in the spring.

MIGHTY ANTLERS

In the summer reindeer eat grass and lichen, but in winter they often head for the shelter of the forest. Female reindeer are unusual as they grow antlers like the males.

WHO DOES WHAT?!!

1. WHICH BIRD'S NEST IS LITTERED WITH FISH BONES ?
   a) Barn owl
   b) Lammergeier
   c) Kingfisher
   d) Andean condor

2. WHICH MALE FISH TAKES CARE OF ITS EGGS?
   a) Stickleback
   b) Goldfish
   c) Piranha
   d) Great white

3. WHICH BIRD SOUNDS LIKE A TRUMPET?
   a) Wood stork
   b) Whooping crane
   c) Snow goose
   d) Barn owl

4. WHICH MONKEY CAN HANG FROM ITS TAIL?
   a) Squirrel monkey
   b) Orangutan
   c) Spider monkey
   d) Anaconda

5. WHICH BABY SHARK IS STRIPED?
   a) Great white shark
   b) Zebra shark
   c) Blacktip reef shark
   d) Hammerhead

6. WHICH ANIMALS BREACH?
a) Sharks
b) Jaguars
c) Whales
d) Lizards

9. WHICH ANIMAL IS FAMOUS FOR ITS BIG APPETITE?
a) Orangutan
b) Camel
c) Wolverine
d) Moose

7. WHICH ANIMAL IS THE BIGGEST?
a) Great white shark
b) Blue whale
c) Marine iguana
d) Zebra

10. WHICH ANIMAL USES ITS TUSKS TO DIG FOR SHELLFISH?
a) Walrus
b) Reindeer
c) Frilled lizard
d) Dolphin

8. WHICH BIRD CAN RUN FASTER THAN AN OLYMPIC RUNNER?
a) Snowy owl
b) Little green heron
c) Roseate spoonbill
d) Ostrich

Answers
1. c; 2. a; 3. b; 4. c; 5. b; 6. c; 7. b; 8. d; 9. d; 10. a.

Index